Whispers in the Wind

Raja Chakraborty

HAWAKAL

HAWAKAL

Published by Hawakal Publishers
185 Kali Temple Road, Nimta, Kolkata 700049
India

Email info@hawakal.com
Website www.hawakal.com

First edition August, 2019

Copyright © Raja Chakraborty 2019

Cover image: Shutterstock
Designed by Bitan Chakraborty

All rights reserved. No part of this publication may be reproduced or transmitted (other than for purposes of review/critique) in any form or by any means, electronic or mechanical, including photocopy, recording, or any information storage and retrieval system without prior permission in writing from the publisher or the copyright holder where applicable. The author asserts his moral right to be identified as the author of his work.

ISBN: 978-93-87883-76-5

Price: 300 INR | USD 8.99

to the memory of my *father*
who taught me to live

CONTENTS

A Day in the Life of a Butcher	9
A Forgotten Love Song	10
Abandoned	11
As Love Passes By	12
Birth of a Poem	13
Bunch of Keys	14
Burdened	15
Camouflage	16
Come Let Me Love You	17
Death by the Waters	18
Death of a Poem	19
Death, My Friend	20
Deconstruction	21
Deep Down	22
Diwali	23
Dream Lover	24
Fairy Tale Stories	25
Fire	26
Forecast	27
Going Away	28
Home Coming	29
In the Blink of an Eye	30
Language of Pain	31

Left Alone	32
Life by the Rivers	33
Lost	34
Love	35
Martyrs	36
Meeting God	37
Nirvana	38
Now and Then	39
Of Echoes and Icicles	40
Of Egos and Bubbles	41
Of Faith	42
Of Lies and Truth	43
Of Love	44
Of Pillars	45
Of Simplicity	46
Of Wings and Winds	47
One Day	48
Peace	49
Perceptions	50
Reflections	52
Rivers	53
Seeds	54
Separation	55
Serendipity	56
Smile with Me	57
Sorry, Said the Flowers	58
Soul Speak	59
Spoils of War	60
Stones	61
Story of a Railway Track	62
The Clothes Line	63
The First Leaf	64
The Forest and I	65

The Leap	66
The Living Dead	67
The Missing	68
The Morning After	70
The Promise	71
The Sunflower Trail	72
The Tunnel	73
The Vampire	74
The Well Within	75
Touchdown	76
Violated	77
When Time Stood Still	78
Whispers in the Wind	79

A Day in the Life of a Butcher

As the skin broke
The truncheon heaved
A sigh of relief
The hand with a heavy heart
Sought refuge in blood
All in a day's work
The mind muttered
To nobody in particular
And readied the next one
In line
With dead eyes
Of a mutilated fish
The head intact

A Forgotten Love Song

I once stole a song for you
From a blue bird
That a summer breeze sang
To the rain clouds
And gave it to your river

Do the waves remember
Still
Do you dance with the wind
Anymore

Abandoned

Doors closed
Windows shut
The house stood
Like a recluse

In memory
Of the smiles
That once lit up
Its many rooms

As Love Passes By

I've got twenty-four hours
To say Love You and
Goodbye

For she is a transient moment
Between this sunrise
And the next

Birth of a Poem

As the last light of a tired day
Vanished behind an obscure horizon
She lit a fire to feed the passions

And a poet found a line of poetry
Draped in beautiful words
To transcend the mundane

Thus a flower bloomed
Amongst the dead winter snow

Bunch of Keys

Standing on the doorsteps of love
A hesitant heart fumbled with a
Bunch of keys

Some keys were lost
Some words were left unspoken

Burdened

Her words
Were pregnant

A few months more
She said

My patience
Impatient always

Cut them out
In caesarian hurry

Blood on my hands
And ghost of the unborn

I carry since
Forever burdened

Camouflage

Shut your eyes
And see the world
In all its nakedness

Camouflage is a game
We all play

Come Let Me Love You

Come let me give you
All my warmth
Let me fill all your emptiness
With sunshine and love
Let all that is mine be yours
I ask for nothing in return
Only a whispered kiss
In a rainy night
Under the stars
I can call my own forever

Death by the Waters

Have you ever thrown
A pebble
To dissolve your
Picture in the water?

To die in them
For lingering moments

Like you die everyday
In so many stories

Life writes for you

Death of a Poem

The night when stars were
In hiding
A callous moon in a pale
Yellow shroud
Faltered in its orbit
And a lonely wind sang a
Sad song
She left unnoticed
Leaving the door open

A poem died
With her receding footsteps

Death, My Friend

When death finally came
It was like a long lost friend
Turning up at your door step
One unsuspecting morning to
Stop by and say hello
And I told myself
Can't let him go alone again
So we walk together these days
Hand in hand, smiling
And talk about life

Deconstruction

I will break myself
Down someday
Into little fragments
Of tiny images
New born moments
Tissue by tissue
I will sketch a canvas
Each stroke a beginning
Each step the first stroll
On a road I have walked
So many times before
Block by block
I will construct
Adonis and Adam
To break them down again

Deep Down

Backwaters of Kerala
A mind with hidden layers
Slowly ate me up
Head to toe
Like the lady of the serpents
And submerged in her
Depths I found
Heartaches sleeping
At her feet
With fragments of
Unfinished love stories
That fishes fed on
To become mermaids
In colored dreams

Diwali

A solitary star
In a lonely sky
Floating aimlessly
In the restless breeze
Found your eyes
To rest for the night

You looked up
And it was
A festival of lights

Dream Lover

As the night fell on her eyes
Dreams were woven
Where the prince lived in a
Shared room with a heart as
Deep as their village river
And she swam the depths to
Find the pearls he had stored
For them
One for each year
They had travelled the roads
In her mind

Fairy Tale Stories

One day I will write
A fairy tale
In bright colors
And laughter

Until then
My bleeding pen
Will speak of
Forgotten tears

Fire

Fire is a voracious omnivore
Insatiable in its hunger
Self-consuming in its greed
It stops at nothing and there
Is no end to it

Ask the forest who has seen
Years and years of labor
Gone to flames in a minute
To the last grass

Ask a soul blackened to a
Dead night that once danced with it

Forecast

Her upturned lips told
Me of a storm coming
Her kohl lined eyes
Spoke of dark clouds
I prepared for the rains

The radio blaring a
Bright sunny day and
A gentle breeze

Going Away

When you go up in vapor
You know that you are
Losing parts of you

And like the falling leaf
You try and hold on
To your last bit

Home Coming

A moth-eaten sky
Hung low over his head
As he walked toward the endless
Grey of a fading horizon

A thin line separating him from
The warmth of a faraway cottage
And a home fire burning

Still fresh in his mind
Like yesterday

Or his other lives
He keeps coming back to

In the Blink of an Eye

Between now and then
A life-time passed

Like the name of a railway station
You missed from the train window

And will never go back to

Language of Pain

Is there a language in which pain cries
Are the words traumatised and
Shaken, scared to come out

Do only eyes that see beyond
Understand them

And decode
In secret silence

Left Alone

Falling from the sky
A raging comet cried tears of fire

Its trail leaving a dark scar
Blacker than the darkness of souls

Left alone to perish
Cosmic graffiti, unadorned

Life by the Rivers

A golden glow
Silently merged with
The twilight darkened river

The last boat
Hurrying home
Rode the impatient waves

A silent pair of eyes
Searched the darkness
For a familiar splash
Of homecoming
Against the black waters

Pangs of unanswered prayers
The banks knew too well

Lost

Tonight, as the sun goes down
For one last time,
I will write my saddest lines
Etched in a night sky,
Dark, deep, blank,
Not a single star to mourn
The demise of a wilted moon
Erased from the memory, only
The faint flicker of a dying
Meteor will carry my words into
Oblivion to rest in the
Crevices of a saddened sky, blue
Turning to the grey of your grief

Love

Love is like a caterpillar
Waiting to be a butterfly

Some get their wings
Some in their shell die

Martyrs

In the battlefield of mind
Emotions die every day
In the name of pride

Unsung martyrs of self
At the altar of life

Meeting God

I met God,
Dressed in a smile
And kindness

Hello, he said,
Come, let's live

Nirvana

When you know what and where your
Senses are
Like you know exactly which jar contains
Cumin seeds or chili flakes on the
Kitchen shelf
Or how many spoonful, as Ma said, is
Needed for the curry
Know that you are almost there in the
Garden
Where Nirvana is a flower
To be sensed, not seen

Now and Then

Traveling backward
I looked ahead
And saw myself

In the same old house
Of mud and steel

A thousand years
Gone in between

Of Echoes and Icicles

Echoes murmur fading sounds
Of broken words
Left alone to float in
Mountain winds
Line of pines
Keeper of alien secrets
Store them in their folds to pass
On to the next traveler

To take home stories of shadows
That walked this
Lonely path and left a last sigh
Frozen in frost

We call icicles

Of Egos and Bubbles

When your image
Grows bigger
Than you,
Awestruck mirror
Put to shame,
You lose entity
And become a
Shadow with
No anchor,
Floating aimlessly
On a bloated ego
Mid-air, clueless
A bubble
Waiting to burst

Of Faith

Soaked in the palette
Of a fading sunset
A tiny flower blushed

And opened its heart
To a roving bee

Of Lies and Truth

They carried him
In the caravan of gods
Draped in pristine whites

To cover all the lies he lived
So truth can survive

Of Love

A refugee
Older than time
Love seeks
Bleeding hearts
To rest for
The night

A parasite
Feeding on grief
Of the unsuspecting

Of Pillars

Let me talk of pillars today
Standing tall and stubborn
Carrying weight of untold sins
In their stone-heart urn
They stand in silent somber lines
Through the storms and age
Weather beaten to the core
Like Atlas the solemn sage
Holding up skies and roofs
And all our sordid lies
We sink a little more in ground
When a pillar dies

Of Simplicity

I wrote a line
No curvatures and no angles
Just a simple straight line
Going from here to there
No stops in between

You tutored by years of
Suspicion and geometry
Of impossible words
Looked for hidden bends
In linear simplicity

And wandered in
The wilderness of circles
Going round and round and
Further away to lose yourself
In the intricate patterns of
A puzzle imagined

Of Wings and Winds

I do not hold grudge against
The wind

Unruly or timid
Full of lust and insinuation
It urged me to cross the line
And fly

Soaring high
On flapping wings

I fear to look down and see
What mayhem I left behind

One Day

A time will come I am sure
When the sun will shine
In right earnest

The deepest corners will
Brighten up to light like
Never before

To smile away the
Encroaching shadows

A new day will be
Born to freedom

Peace

Not wanting to talk reason
To them anymore
I took a drag on my cigar
Puffed logic into thin air
And dipped myself in the
Whisky pool

Looking for an ocean
Yet to be disturbed

Perceptions

Every chair was taken
They waited in a tense hush
The curtains began their
Ritual parting

A single spotlight
Its beam firm and narrow
Made a perfect circle
Centre stage

And there he stood
Head down
Arms stretched
Like he had every day
And night
All his life

Some saw a father
Some a mother
Some a child

And each carried
A part of the
Picture they drew
Back home

To make their own stories
Of a man standing alone
To embrace all suffering

Or a woman
Or child

Reflections

When the light goes
Do you see darkness
Playing it out in shades of grey,
Fuzzy shadows dance
Itching to touch the next
In fading lines, shy,
Black corridors with no
Boundaries, walls dissolving
In charcoal depths
An unending streak, it
Goes on, till your eyes open
Up and you see yourself
Standing at the far end,
Stark naked, bereft of all
That you thought was you,
An alien silhouette
That you are afraid now
To call your own

Rivers

Let the rivers flow
From end to end
Undeterred

Let them teach your
Little ones to swim
And ride the waves

So they do not drown
In their own tears

Seeds

Someday
Somewhere
A seed will
Wake up
To be a leaf

And a poem
Will be born

Separation

I never asked
Why you did not come back

For me
You never left

Your fragrance
Still makes my flowers heady

Your words
Still make poetry

Serendipity

Serendipity, a voluptuous myth
A dreamer's convoluted dream
Fabricated rainbow, where there's none,
Stopped me dead in my track one
Uneven autumn morning, whiff of a
Cold greyness hanging in the miffed air.
Hidden in the foliage of a single
Mahogany, nestled between branches
That hardly saw eye to eye, sat my
Lost pair of spectacles, with a lopsided
Grin. Isn't it a miracle that miracles
Still happen, when you almost lost faith.
To find your vision and spectacles,
In the exact same moment, is no less
A magical act than that of Moses,
Which brought a divine smile on ocean
Lips and they parted, in utter surprise.

Smile with Me

Seconds and minutes mourn lost time
Hours, they go by

Lying alone on a stretcher, cold
My soul's waiting to die

Lonely web, broken and bruised
Plays the storm, still brave

You'll see a smile you know so well
If you ever come to my grave

Don't bring flowers or light a candle
Let slicence and darkness be

Touch the stone and if you can
Just smile along with me

Sorry, Said the Flowers

And so she went
Tears swallowed with pride
Her head held high
Not turning even half back to look
At the years spent together

And here I am
Cocooned in a corner
Shut in the hard shell of ego
Mouthing nothingness in the air
As my heart pumped empty

The bougainvillea she planted
Blooms every morning now
I count the flowers into so many
Sorrys I could have said to her

Soul Speak

Have you heard flowers blooming
In silent melody, each petal
A symphony of desire

Have you ever listened to the
Music of fallen leaves, whispering
Notes of surrender

Have you heard the wandering
Clouds, humming forgotten tunes
Of love, in harmony

I have heard them all
In your eyes, in your smile
In your tender sighs

And made them my own
Sacred serenades to you, soul
To soul, floating in the wind

Spoils of War

A splash of red on a winter highway
A lonely boot, lying dead center, ownerless
Smell of burnt flesh and gunpowder
Fighting the fragrance of goulash

Faraway, in a hot, sultry village by the sea
A woman sat motionless, sculpted in
Stoney grief

Her newborn suckling at her swollen
Breast, unmindful of all mayhem

It's snowing again, all will be white
In a while

Stones

Ripped from the heart
Mind metamorphoses
Through sorrow, grief
Anger and pain to turn
Into stones that litter
The path of our existence

Eons later a curious
Geologist or a son or
Daughter will dig into our
Earth to find them and
Shed a tear perhaps

And a soul will rest
In happiness finally
Knowing that stones have
Hearts after all

Story of a Railway Track

Like jilted lovers
They ran
Side by side
Connected by
Unseen roots
Never touching

Into the
Wilderness

For a destination
Unknown

The Clothes Line

A motley collection of shirts
And trousers left hanging
On the clothes line
Waiting for the sun and a
Favorable wind to dry up

Morose and sagging
With the weight of dead skin
Shedding tears

Threads carrying
Memories of a man
Who walked into a night and
Forgot to see the sunrise

The First Leaf

A yellow morning and
An empty sky
Life dragging on
Monotones of a sepia hue
A dull drone slowly
Killing the music

And then the first leaf
Of a new spring
Opened its hazel eyes

I smiled knowing
Every end is a beginning

The Forest and I

The moss grew on me
Inching its way up
Slow in its climb

Earth will be reclaimed
The day nothing of
Me is left

And I am one
With the forest

The Leap

Let go my hand
Trust your wings, float
Make friends with the wind,
Head cocked to a side
The little sparrow
Listened to its mother,
Eyes wide open with fear
And faith, it fluttered
Its tentative tiny wings,
Gathering courage and
Momentum, bobbing on the
Branch that was its world
So long and letting it go,
Spiralling down, wings flapping,
She hugged the unknown air
Like a mother's bosom, to
Fly away into a sky, her own

The Living Dead

Learn to breathe
Else life is such a
Hollow time

A dead watch
You found in the closet
And wondered
When the day passed
In silence

The Missing

Cigarette smoke
Heavy in the air
Whiff of single malt
Matured
Amber touching gold
Pages of The Missing
Fluttering on the table
Mahogany it seemed
Inherited
Like the uncertain
Tomorrow
And a nonchalant
Today
He sat looking
At the wall
And faces from the
Past looked back
At him
His many lives
That sat on the same
Rocking chair
Through years of solitude

And madness
The clock
Silent in its grief
Ticked on
And counted
Missing blocks
Lost in the name
Of sanity

The Morning After

A half-hearted night
Knocked into a reluctant dawn

A weary moon whispered hello
To a sleeping sun

And I saw a morning in the haze
Of a drunkard's veil

In a slow motion blur
Drifting

The Promise

A dull summer day
Boiled in an airless
Stifling heat

The afternoon slowly
Decomposed into
A stale night

And a jaundiced moon
Smelling of sweat
Struggled in a grey sky

To breathe love
Promised to a dying star
Lost in a black hole

The Sunflower Trail

I walked her
Footsteps
Warmth of soil
On my feet
Bifurcating the
Sunflowers
Yellow sea of
Her memories
From buds
To blossom
They tell
Her story
Every fallen
Petal her face
For she lived
In the flowers

The Tunnel

Every day is a trap
Bright images to allure
Music in the corridor
And a deep drag
To suck you in
A bottomless pit
Of no return

The tunnel growing
Heavy on me

I travel in dark nights
To search for light

The Vampire

A vicious smile like cancer
Spread on his corrupt lips
As he smelled blood in her
Naked skin, warm and fresh
His glazed eyes, soaked in
Frenzy, burned into her soul
He sunk his hungry teeth
In her untouched innocence

And with her tears he wrote
One more flower gone
One more grave to dig

The Well Within

Born in the
Land of draughts

She cried
To quench the thirst
Of her new born
And wash
Her husband's
Plate of grief

With the broken
Waters of a
Lost child

As the rivers
Flow wasted
In an alien land

Touchdown

Tranquility prevails
Thirty-five thousand
Above sea level
In an airtight cabin

Wheel touching ground
Reality hits with
A vengeance

An earthquake
Sans warning

Violated

Stripped of her cover
And shame
She lay bare on
The roadside

Passing headlights
Caught her in
Fragments of
Hapless nudity

Eyes frozen she was
Watching her own
Blood in amazement
Trickling between
Her thrown-apart legs

She forgot to cry
Instead sought warmth
In the stray dog
Licking her face
With tear filled eyes
Mouthing a silent sorry
If only we could

When Time Stood Still

A moment
Paused

I saw an
Eternal sunset
In your eyes

And a night
For ever

Whispers in the Wind

And so she said
One autumn evening
As the trees were shedding
And the wind played truant

Come lie next to me
Let your warmth be my skin
Let my soul touch yours forever

Let my eyes speak to you of a
Love that words failed

And so she said
One autumn evening
As the last spark of a dying fire
Sighed and went out

www.ingramcontent.com/pod-product-compliance
Lightning Source LLC
Chambersburg PA
CBHW031458040426
42444CB00007B/1142